The Mighty World of
EMERGENCY VEHICLES

The Mighty World of

EMERGENCY VEHICLES

FOG
CITY

PRESS

Published by Fog City Press,
a division of Weldon Owen Inc.
1045 Sansome Street
San Francisco, CA 94111 USA

www.weldonowen.com

weldon**owen**
President & Publisher Roger Shaw
Associate Publisher Mariah Bear
SVP, Sales & Marketing Amy Kaneko
Finance Manager Philip Paulick
Editor Bridget Fitzgerald
Creative Director Kelly Booth
Art Director Meghan Hildebrand
Senior Production Designer Rachel Lopez Metzger
Production Director Chris Hemesath
Associate Production Director Michelle Duggan
Director of Enterprise Systems Shawn Macey
Imaging Manager Don Hill

Library of Congress Control Number on file with the publisher.

ISBN 13: 978-1-68188-098-3
ISBN 10: 1-68188-098-9

10 9 8 7 6 5 4 3 2 1

2016 2017 2018 2019

Printed by 1010 Printing in China.

We need help right away when there's an emergency. That's when ambulances, fire trucks, and police cars come to the rescue. Their flashing lights and loud sirens warn people that they are in a hurry.

But what happens when there's an emergency high in the mountains or far out at sea? The emergency services have it covered, and helicopters, sleds, and boats carry people to safety. It's time to fasten your seatbelt and watch some amazing rescue vehicles in action.

When the fire alarm rings, these fire engines are ready to go. Signals inside the station can even make traffic lights turn red to stop traffic. Off they go!

FUN FACT
The first fire truck was just a hand pump on wheels!

Police vehicles are on the alert, too. In any kind of emergency, the police are ready all around the world.

FUN FACT
Police cars have many nicknames, like "panda cars."

FUN FACT
Many retired police vehicles become collectors' items!

Police motorcycles can move quickly on busy city streets and highways. They can fit into narrow spaces where cars can't travel.

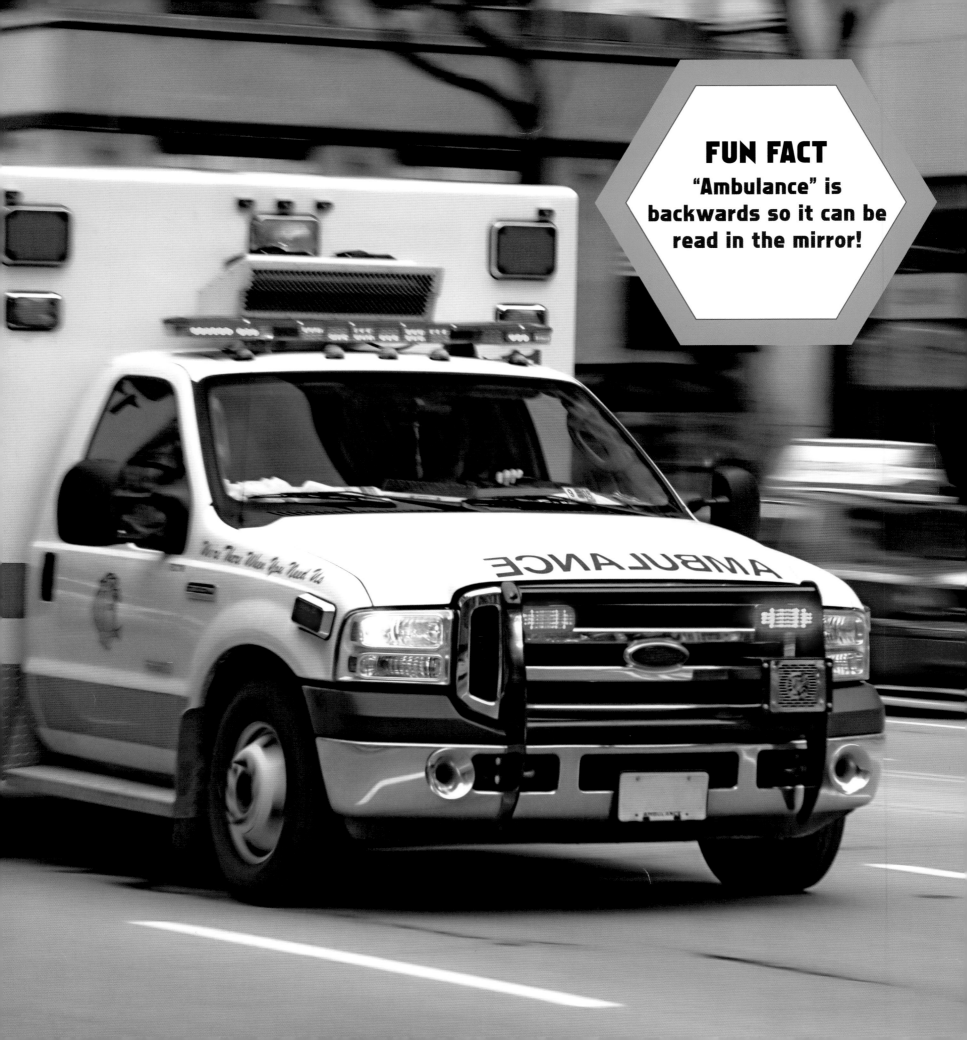

FUN FACT
"Ambulance" is backwards so it can be read in the mirror!

Ambulances are in charge of transporting the sick and wounded.

Rescue workers arrive with their equipment. A pumper truck pumps water from a fire hydrant.

FUN FACT
Fire trucks can be all colors, like red, yellow, white, green, or black.

FUN FACT

Police officers and firefighters work together in a crisis.

Each rescue worker has a specific job to do—such as helping an injured person or hosing down a fire.

The inside of an ambulance is like a moving emergency room, with equipment for transporting an injured person to the hospital.

FUN FACT
Ambulances can be vans, boats, trucks, and even bicycles.

Helicopters can hover, or stay in one place, in the air. They can patrol the scene from the skies.

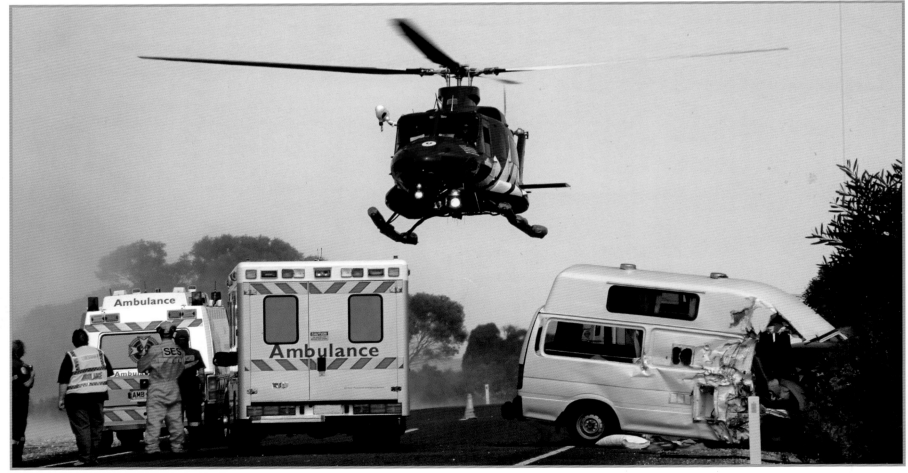

FUN FACT

Helicopters can fly as fast as 248 mph (400 kph).

FUN FACT
Helicopters are sometimes called choppers.

Air ambulances can land in difficult spots and quickly carry people away to safety.

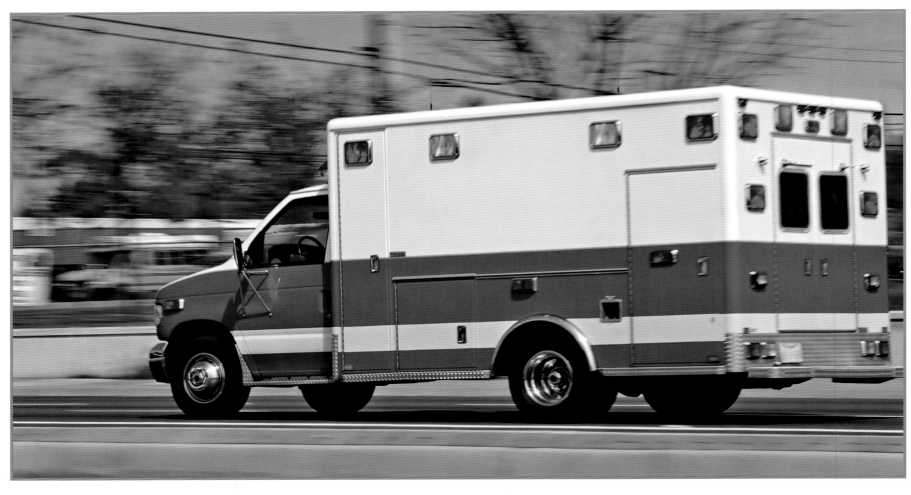

Sirens on! The blue
symbol on some
ambulances
is called the
"star of life."

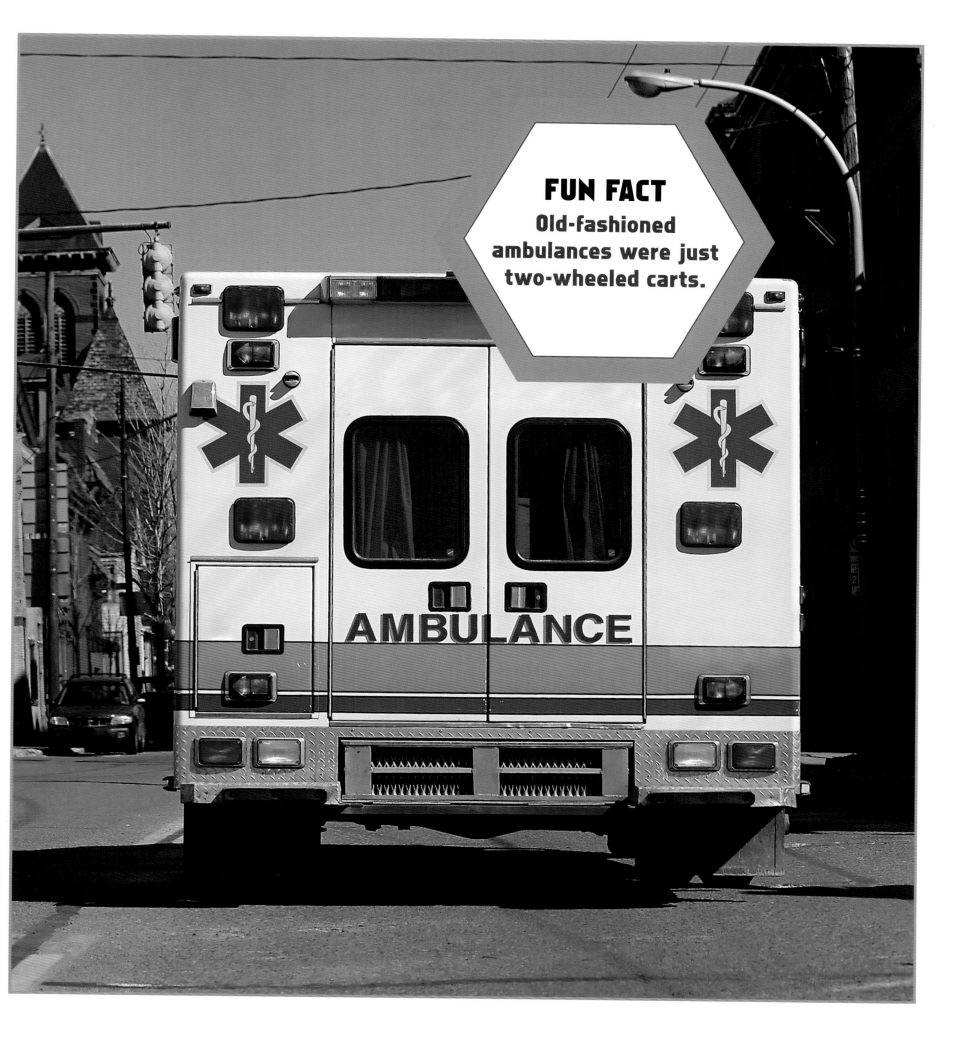

FUN FACT
Old-fashioned ambulances were just two-wheeled carts.

FUN FACT
Pumper trucks pump water from hydrants, pools, or lakes.

At the scene of a fire, three types of fire trucks can arrive: pumper trucks, tanker trucks, and ladder trucks.

FUN FACT
Ladder trucks carry firefighters to the top floors of buildings.

Special knobs on
the truck control
the water power.
The inside of a
fire truck is like
a giant toolbox.

Fire-fighting helicopters drop water or foam from tanks or buckets onto wildfires.

FUN FACT
Hovering is a difficult skill for the pilot to learn.

FUN FACT
Fire-fighting foam cools the fire and cuts off the fuel source.

Airports have fire engines called "crash tenders." Their nozzles send out jets of water or foam to put out airplane fires.

What about when there's a fire at sea? Fireboats shoot out water from huge pumps and nozzles.

FUN FACT
Even inflatable rescue
boats (IRBs) can climb
huge waves.

The bright orange rescue boat is easy to spot in the ocean or river. It can go out in water too rough for most boats.

If you're in trouble in the water, a lifeguard can ride a personal watercraft to reach you.

Police and coast guard crews use boats to rescue people and to patrol the waters.

FUN FACT
The coast guard was founded over 200 years ago!

FUN FACT
Helicopters are used for photography, tourism, and searches.

High in the mountains, helicopters send rescuers down by rope and pull people up again.

In the snowy tundra, sleds, snowmobiles, and all-terrain vehicles can also come to the rescue.

FUN FACT
Snowmobiles can handle rough terrain to access remote areas.